Simple Machines

Wedges
and ramps

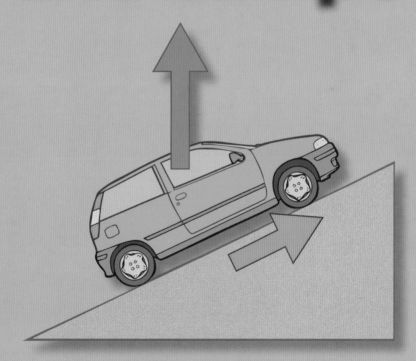

Chris Oxlade

Smart Apple Media

Published by Smart Apple Media
2140 Howard Drive West
North Mankato, MN 56003

Designed by Helen James
Edited by Mary-Jane Wilkins
Artwork by Bill Donohoe

Photographs by
page 5 Jim Zuckerman/Corbis; 6 Keren Su/Corbis; 10 Hein van den
Heuvel/Zefa/Corbis; 12 Rosa & Rosa/Corbis; 15 Jim Craigmyle/Corbis;
16 Chris Oxlade; 17 Jessica Rinaldi/Reuters/Corbis; 18 Klaus Hackenberg/
Zefa/Corbis; 20 Helmut Mayer Zur Capellen/Zefa/Corbis; 21 Linda
Richardson/Corbis; 22 Maurice Nimmo; Frank Lane Picture Agency/Corbis;
23 Michael Nicholson/Corbis; 28 Ben Le/Corbis; 29 Laureen March/Corbis

Printed in China

Library of Congress Cataloging-in-Publication Data

Oxlade, Chris.
Wedges and ramps / by Chris Oxlade.
p. cm. — (Simple machines)
Includes index.
ISBN 978-1-59920-086-6
1. Simple machines—Juvenile literature. 2. Inclined planes—Juvenile literature.
3. Wedges—Juvenile literature. I. Title.

TJ147.O88 2007
621.8—dc22   2007004881

First Edition

9 8 7 6 5 4 3 2 1

Contents

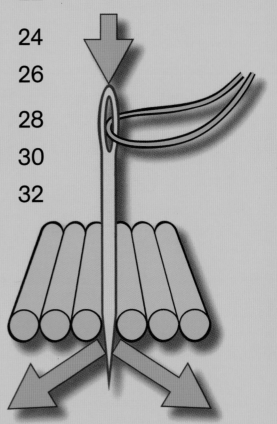

What is a simple machine?

A simple machine is something that helps you do a job. We use simple machines to help us every day. Here are some simple machines you might have at home.

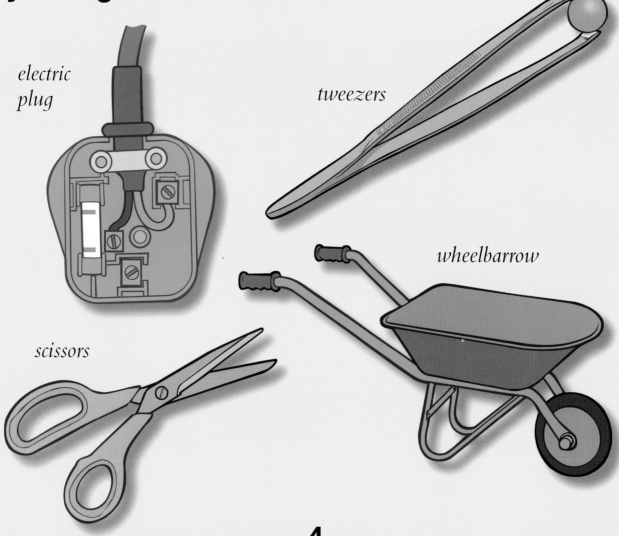

electric plug

tweezers

wheelbarrow

scissors

This book is about simple machines called wedges and ramps.

The head of an ax is a wedge that is used to cut wood. A ramp is like a wedge. It helps lift things.

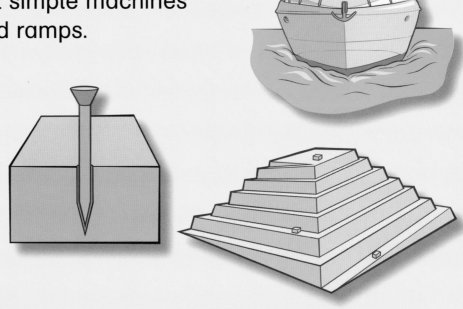

The head of an ax is wedge-shaped.

Pushes and pulls

You push on a wedge to make it work. When you push, the wedge makes a push, too. Scientists call all pushes and pulls "forces."

This chisel is a wedge. A stonemason shapes stone with a chisel.

On paper, arrows are used to show pushes and pulls. The arrow points in the direction of the pushing or pulling force. A longer arrow means a bigger push or pull.

Red arrows show pushes and pulls.

Blue arrows show movement.

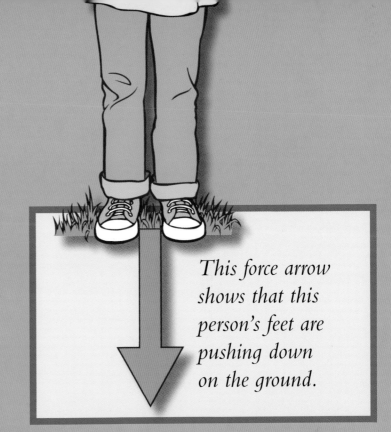

This force arrow shows that this person's feet are pushing down on the ground.

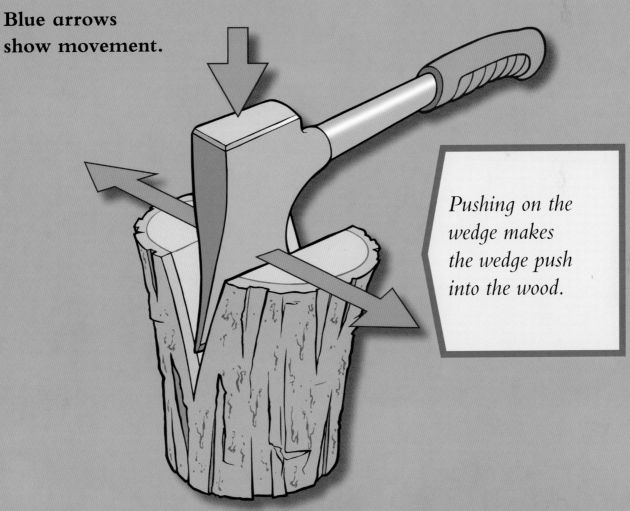

Pushing on the wedge makes the wedge push into the wood.

How wedges and ramps work

A wedge is a simple machine. It is made from hard material, such as wood, plastic, or metal. From the side, it is shaped like a triangle.

A wedge changes the direction of a push. It makes the push larger, too.

A ramp is a wedge that lies on the ground. A ramp doesn't move. Instead, you push something up a ramp. This is easier than lifting the object straight up.

Pushing an object up a ramp is a way of lifting it higher.

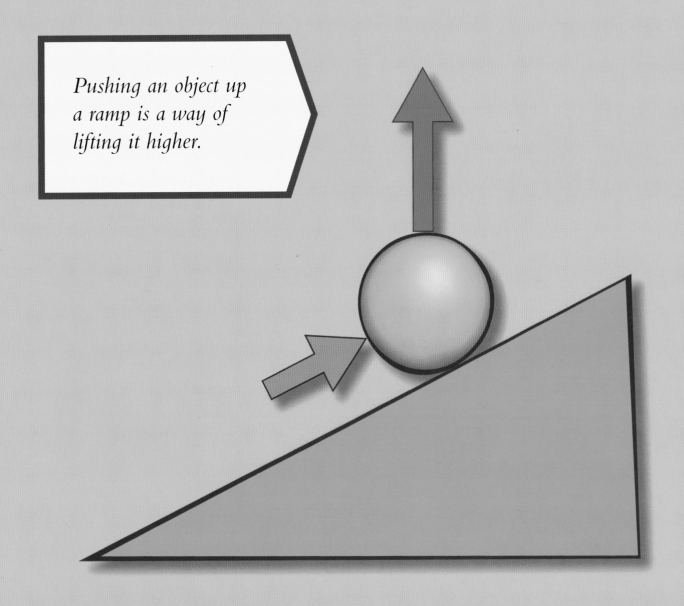

Cutting with wedges

We use wedges to cut materials.
A pizza cutter has a wedge
around the outside of the wheel.

You press the pizza cutter down
and roll it. The wedge cuts the pizza
and pushes the pieces apart.

A pizza cutter works like a rolling knife.

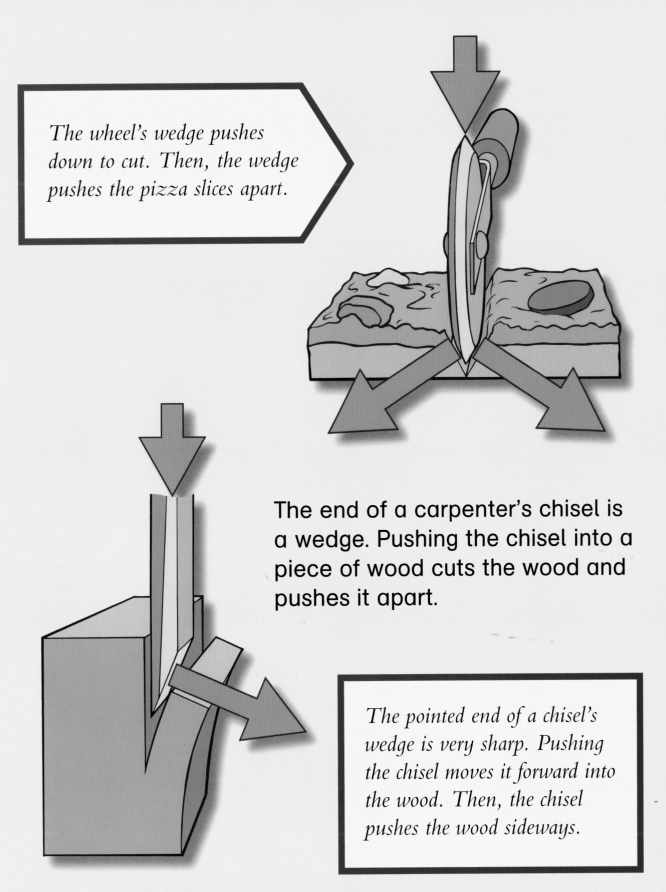

The wheel's wedge pushes down to cut. Then, the wedge pushes the pizza slices apart.

The end of a carpenter's chisel is a wedge. Pushing the chisel into a piece of wood cuts the wood and pushes it apart.

The pointed end of a chisel's wedge is very sharp. Pushing the chisel moves it forward into the wood. Then, the chisel pushes the wood sideways.

Piercing with wedges

We use wedges to pierce materials and to make holes.

The sharp point of a nail is a wedge. The wedge pushes wood to the side as the nail is hammered in.

Hammering a nail makes a large force that splits the wood.

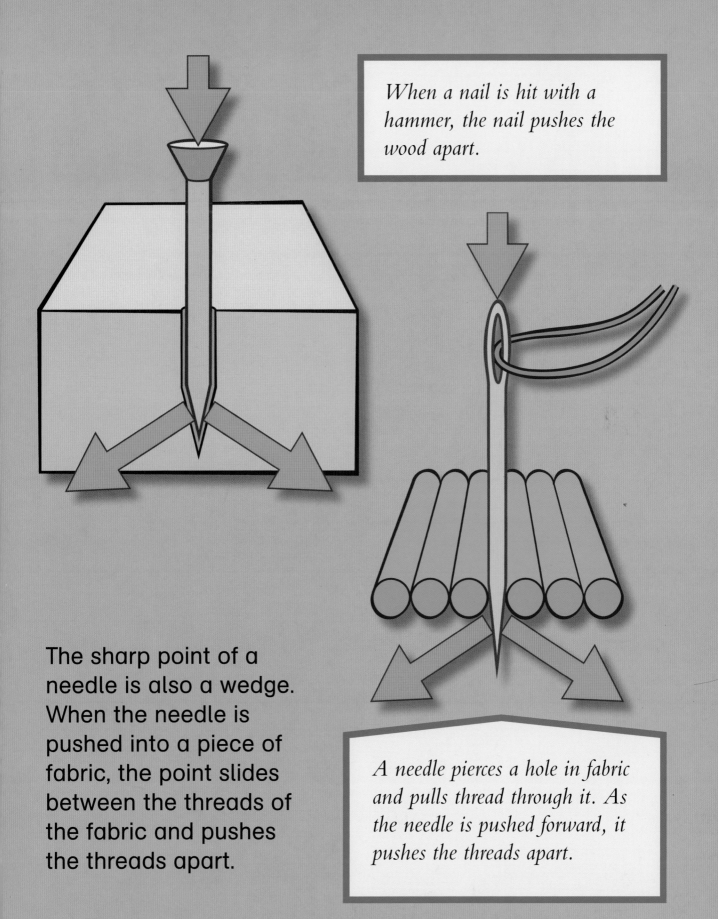

When a nail is hit with a hammer, the nail pushes the wood apart.

The sharp point of a needle is also a wedge. When the needle is pushed into a piece of fabric, the point slides between the threads of the fabric and pushes the threads apart.

A needle pierces a hole in fabric and pulls thread through it. As the needle is pushed forward, it pushes the threads apart.

Gripping with wedges

We can force wedges into gaps to grip things and keep them from moving.

A door wedge holds a door open when we force it between the door and the floor.

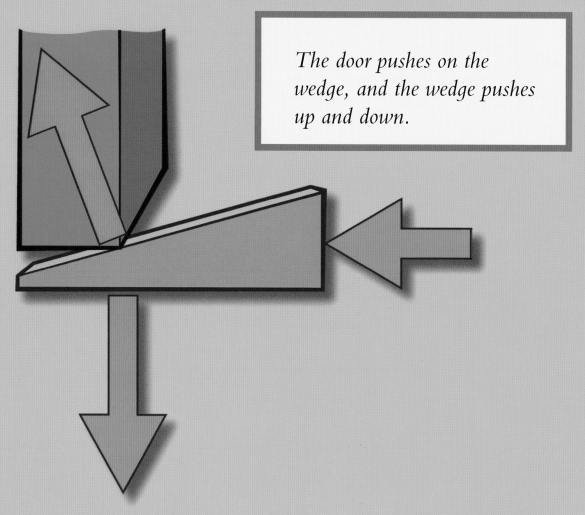

The door pushes on the wedge, and the wedge pushes up and down.

Carpenters use wedges in joints that connect pieces of wood. A wedge forces the pieces tightly together so that they can't move apart.

A carpenter puts together a dovetail joint. This joint has two wedges in the middle.

Lifting with ramps

Ramps make it easier to move things higher.

A loading ramp makes it easier to lift heavy things onto a vehicle. It would be much harder to lift them straight up without a ramp.

A backhoe is loaded onto a trailer by driving it up a ramp.

A wheelchair ramp allows people who use wheelchairs to enter a building from the sidewalk. The ramp has a very gradual slope so that people can push themselves up it.

This person uses a ramp to get to his front door.

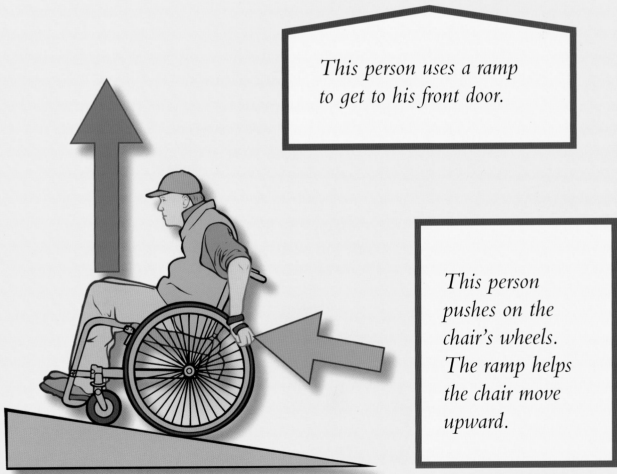

This person pushes on the chair's wheels. The ramp helps the chair move upward.

More ramps

We use ramps on paths, roads, and railroads. Ramps make it easier to move up hills.

A zigzag path is a ramp that makes it easier to walk up a steep hill. Going straight up a hill is much harder.

A staircase is a ramp. It is easier to walk up stairs than to climb straight up a ladder.

Most cars and trucks cannot go up very steep hills. Their engines do not have enough force and the wheels slip. They need ramps to help them go up hills.

The car's wheels push the car forward. The ramp helps the car move upward.

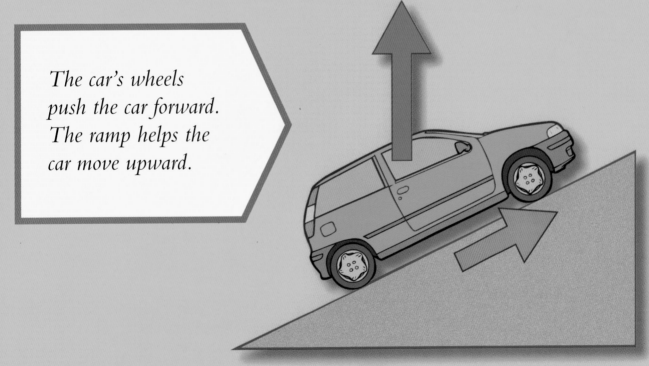

Wedges and ramps in machines

Complicated machines often use wedges and ramps to work.

A backhoe's bucket uses wedges to break up the soil. The front of the bucket has wedge-shaped teeth.

As the backhoe's bucket pushes into the ground, its teeth split apart the soil.

The front of a high-speed train has a wedge shape. The wedge pushes the air aside as the train speeds along the track.

A train's wedge-shaped nose pushes air up and over the train.

A quarry conveyor moves crushed rock into a storage building. The conveyor is a ramp.

This conveyor lifts heavy rocks. It would need more force to lift the rocks straight up.

Wedges and ramps in the past

People have been using wedges and ramps for thousands of years.

The wedge was one of the first tools that people used. They made wedge-shaped cutting tools and arrowheads by chipping stones into shape.

A cutting tool made from a hard stone called flint.

The plow was invented thousands of years ago. The first plows were simple, wedge-shaped pieces of wood. When a plow was pulled along the ground, it broke up the soil so that seeds could be planted.

This picture shows people plowing 1,000 years ago.

Builders used ramps before cranes were invented. The Egyptians built huge ramps to move the giant stone blocks for their pyramids.

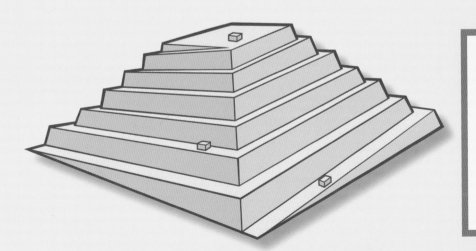

Teams of Egyptian workers pushed and pulled stones up the ramps.

23

Fun with wedges and ramps

The activities on the next four pages will help you understand how wedges and ramps work.

TESTING A WEDGE

You will need:
- a pencil with one flat end and one pointed end
- modeling clay
- a heavy book

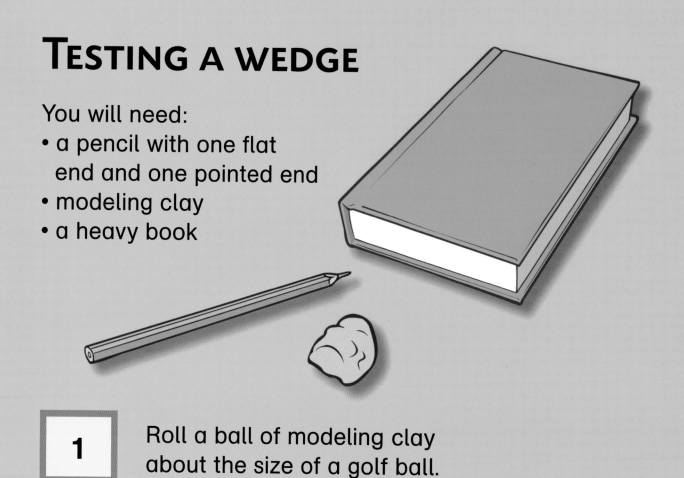

1 Roll a ball of modeling clay about the size of a golf ball.

2 Press down on the ball to flatten its top.

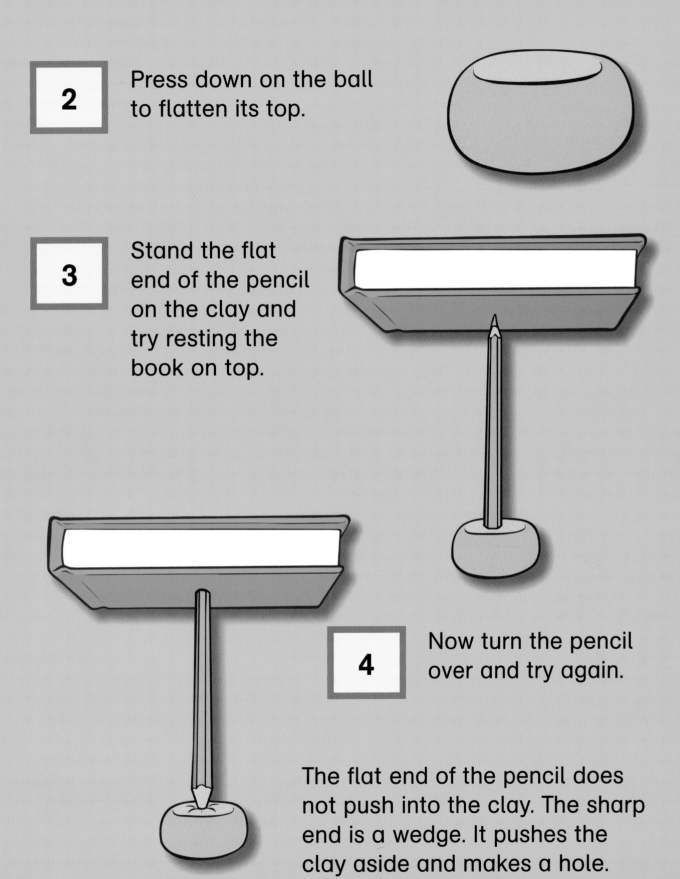

3 Stand the flat end of the pencil on the clay and try resting the book on top.

4 Now turn the pencil over and try again.

The flat end of the pencil does not push into the clay. The sharp end is a wedge. It pushes the clay aside and makes a hole.

Sliding up a ramp

You will need:
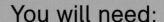
- a thin rubber band
- a piece of string about 20 inches (51 cm) long
- a large book and some small books
- a small, heavy object, such as a stapler

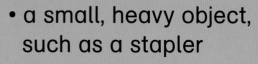

1	Make a stack of books about 4 inches (10 cm) high.

2	Rest one end of the large book on the stack to make a ramp.

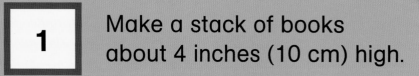

| **3** | Tie one end of the string to the object and the other end to the rubber band. |

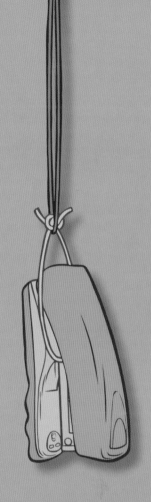

| **4** | Lift the object by pulling on the end of the rubber band. |

| **5** | Rest the object on the ramp and pull it up the ramp by pulling the rubber band. |

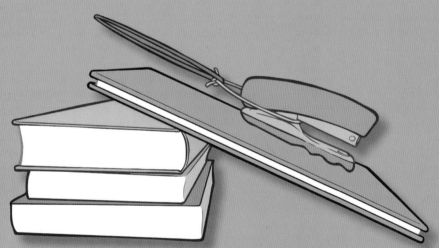

The rubber band stretches more when you lift the object vertically. The ramp lets you use a smaller pull to lift the object.

Find the wedges and ramps

Can you find the wedges and ramps on these pages? Try to figure out what each one does.

Find the wedge. What does it do?

You have wedges in your body! What are they called?

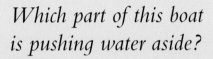

Which part of this boat is pushing water aside?

There are two ramps on a playground slide. Where are they?

Answers are on page 32.

Words to remember

ax
A simple tool with a metal, wedge-shaped head
on a handle that is used for chopping wood.

backhoe bucket
A tool that a backhoe uses to dig holes in
the ground.

carpenter
Someone who makes things from wood.

chisel
A piece of metal with a sharp, wedge-shaped end
that is used for shaping a piece of wood.

conveyor
A machine that moves material, such as crushed
rock, from place to place.

dovetail joint
A way of connecting two pieces of wood.
Dovetail joints are often used in wooden
boxes and furniture.

forces
Pushes or pulls.

hammer
A simple tool used for pushing nails into wood
and also for pulling them out of wood.

plow
A wedge-shaped tool for breaking up the soil
in fields to plant new crops.

pyramid
A building with a square base and a pointed top.

stonemason
Someone who cuts stone
and builds things with it.

zigzag
A pattern that goes from
side to side in short lines.

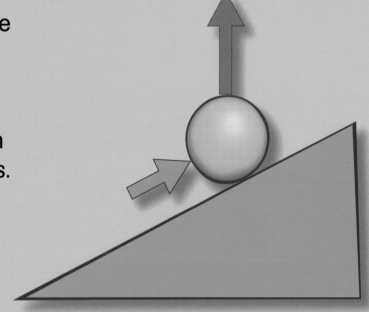

Index

Answers to pages 28–29

The wedge is under the tire. It keeps the plane from moving.
Your teeth are wedges. They cut through food.
The front part of the boat is a wedge that pushes through the water.
The steps on a slide and the slide are both ramps.